W. B. Yeats

by WILLIAM YORK TINDALL

Columbia University Press
NEW YORK & LONDON 1966

COLUMBIA ESSAYS ON MODERN WRITERS is a series of critical studies of English, Continental, and other writers whose works are of contemporary artistic and intellectual significance.

Editor: William York Tindall

Advisory Editors
Jacques Barzun   W. T. H. Jackson   Joseph A. Mazzeo   Justin O'Brien

W. B. Yeats is Number 15 of the series.

WILLIAM YORK TINDALL, Professor of English at Columbia University, and General Editor of this series, is the author of *James Joyce: His Way of Interpreting the World, The Joyce Country, A Reader's Guide to Dylan Thomas, The Literary Symbol, D. H. Lawrence and Susan His Cow, Forces in Modern British Literature;* and *Samuel Beckett* in this series.

Selections from the following titles by William Butler Yeats are used with the permission of The Macmillan Company, New York, Macmillan & Co. Ltd., and the Estate of William Butler Yeats: *Collected Poems, Responsibilities, Later Poems from Michael Roberts and Dancer, The Tower, The Winding Stair, Last Poems and Plays, The Seven Woods, Green Helmet and Other Poems, The Wild Swans at Coole, Collected Plays, Explorations;* Copyright 1903, 1906, 1912, 1916, 1919, 1921, 1924, 1928, 1933, 1934 by The Macmillan Company, renewed 1931, 1934 by William Butler Yeats, 1940, 1944, 1946, 1949, 1952, 1956, 1961, 1962 by Bertha Georgie Yeats.

W. B. Yeats

Yeats is the great poet of our time and, if taste and judgment can be counted on, the greatest poet of the British Isles since Milton's time. From then till now nobody has made of parts so fine so fine a body of verse.

Of embodying Yeats said: "Man can embody truth but he cannot know it." Statements of truth, in Yeats's poems anyway, are often questions. But his embodiments, grand and final, are beyond all question. Our confusions and his own yielded triumphs of measurement and, beyond these, what he called "magnanimities of sound."

"Unity of being," his ideal in life and art, demanded composing a body of poems and recomposing some with that body in mind. Like a mortal body, this system of interacting parts developed and changed through the years. *The Collected Poems*, establishing unity, preserves each evolutionary stage. Early Yeats is at once like and unlike later Yeats. "The Lake Isle of Innisfree" is the vestigial youth of "Sailing to Byzantium." Or, to change Yeats's metaphor of the body for that of the tree, his poems are like a growing tree—a "rooted blossomer." The roots are one but the foliage changes through the four seasons and, after a display of flower and fruit, withers into the truth. However radical the analyst may be, delighting in seasons, he commonly finds three or four in the work of Yeats. Convenience, too, commends division into periods—say, four.

The work of Yeats in all four periods is of several kinds: poems, essays, stories, and plays. Work of each kind may be important, but limits here demand particular notice of the

[3]

poems. Just as well; for whatever the merits of Yeats as a writer of plays and other things, it is his poems that we return to again and again. What closer approach than this to beauty—and truth?

> It's certain that fine women eat
> A crazy salad with their meat.

What happier union of parts?

Unity, escaping him in life, was his in art. Yet his art is made of quarreling opposites—the grand and the common-place, the personal and the impersonal, love and hate of Ire-land—opposites that achieve oneness by a kind of conspiracy. Poems that show our time forth by whatever seems its op-posite—by a noble response to ignobility—are nonetheless of our time, unmistakably. "The Second Coming," though la-menting ceremonies of innocence and recalling their air, has the air as well of a time without ceremony or innocence. Taking a look at time from the porch of timelessness, "Sailing to Byzantium," an artifact of our time, becomes an "artifice of eternity."

Born in Dublin in 1865, Yeats came of a good middle-class family, clergymen (of the Anglican persuasion) on one side, merchants on the other. A man without formal education is not necessarily ignorant. Far from being this, Yeats was for-tunate in having a father who taught him what, for his pur-poses, he had to know. Reputedly the best talker in Dublin, a city of talkers, John Butler Yeats provided respect for words, not only his own but those of Shakespeare, which he read to his son at bedtime. A painter of the pre-Raphaelite school, John Butler Yeats gave the boy the run of his studio, intro-duced him to painters and poets, William Morris among them, and, as a Victorian aesthete had to, gave the boy contempt for the ugly middle class. A gentleman, said Yeats's father, does not push; careless of getting ahead, avoiding the committee room and the corridors of the ticking world, a gentleman despises the "noisy set" of politicians, merchants, scientists, and, above all, journalists. Yeats learned the lesson at his father's knee:

> Should H. G. Wells afflict you
> Put whitewash in a pail;
> Paint: 'Science—opium of the suburbs'
> On some waste wall.

This is old Yeats writing in discouragement. The pity is that young Yeats, who had seen Shaw as a smiling sewing machine, had to earn a living by journalism—and hack work. (Editing the less agreeable works of Blake brought Yeats no money.) To show his opinion of his colleagues he put on a long black cloak which, says George Moore, who came upon the reluctant journalist one day in one of the seven woods at Coole, gave him the appearance of "a huge umbrella left behind by some picnic party."

At Sligo, where Yeats spent the summers with his mother's family, he disported on Ben Bulben and Innisfree. (What happier places for a poet to disport on?) In London, in winter, from the rhymers of The Rhymers' Club, who kept apart from society on Tuesdays or Thursdays at the Cheshire Cheese, Yeats learned of Walter Pater and useless beauty. Two of these Paterites, Lionel Johnson and Arthur Symons, the one austere, the other eager, became his friends. But his women friends of the 1890s were more important: Maud Gonne, Olivia Shakespear (Johnson's cousin and, later, Ezra Pound's mother-in-law), and Lady Gregory, a patron looking for a poet. Of these Maud Gonne was the most obsessive and the least rewarding: "My devotion might as well have been offered to an image in a milliner's window." But this girl, of great beauty and maddening ways, provided the hopeless love a romantic poet needs.

[5]

Around 1885, four years before he met Maud Gonne, Yeats had begun to write poems and plays for the closet, among these *Mosada*, about a Moorish girl and the Spanish inquisition. The verse showed promise, but the subject seemed remote. That Yeats was not altogether careless of reality is proved by "The Happy Shepherd." Here, lamenting the "Grey Truth" of science and, with its triumph, the death of imagination, he finds "words alone" the "certain good." Words spoken into an "echo-harbouring" shell and filling his ear with "melodious guile"—if he can transfer this shell quickly enough from mouth to ear—are the only comfort in a waste where "human truth" has withered under the scientist's "optic glass." (In "The Sad Shepherd" human words, distorted by alien nature, share the fate of words in E. M. Forster's caves.) "Words alone" may still please the happy shepherd, but "alone," an ambiguous word, may mean only, or spoken to oneself, or autonomous. That Yeats did not intend the last of these is sure; for his early words, referential by design, commonly concern Ireland and the occult, which, along with unhappy love, were his obsessions. But their claims, various and incompatible, pulled the lover of unity in three directions.

Ireland for the literary patriot, who abandoned practical politics after the fall of Parnell, was not the Ireland of Joyce's committee room, but a loftier place entirely. Yeats got his idea of Ireland not only from the landscape of Sligo but from John O'Leary, a noble old Fenian, from Standish O'Grady, whose *History of Ireland* displayed heroes, and from old women, crooning of fairies in the chimney corners. To save Ireland from present ignobility by a vision of the past, Yeats wrote ballads and folk songs, collected legends and stories of the little people, and, above all, sang Ireland's ancient heroes, Cuchulain, Fergus, and Oisin, whose example might elevate and unite those whom the verses charmed. But Yeats's "romantic Ireland" of peasant and hero joined Maud Gonne among lost causes. She continued to carry bombs in her reticule and the politicians, indifferent to Cuchulain, continued to squabble. Though aware of waging an "endless war with Irish stupidity," Yeats indefatigably pursued his end. Not the return of Ireland to heroic tradition but several poems—words alone— were the result. The longest of these is "The Wanderings of Oisin" (1889), which, as William Morris saw, is his kind of poetry. Yeats's Oisin loses his strength on returning from three "allegorical dreams" to Irish reality, but Yeats, stronger than his hero, survived his dreams.

Unable to accept the materialism of Huxley or the church of his great-grandfather, the rector of Drumcliff, Yeats found something more to his purpose in the Theosophical Society and, after 1890, the order of Rosicrucians, which offered meaning, ceremony, and a store of ancient images. Rosicrucians, conjuring some spirits up, distilled others in alembics. The "distillation of alchemy," said Yeats, is better than the "analyses of chemistry"; but, however fascinated, he was neither a fanatic nor a fool. His dizziest raptures were qualified by "rather" or "perhaps." Perhaps what detained him in these queer regions was his concern with words. Here, words put on magical power. What is more, the Hermetic occultists, proclaiming the "laws of the imagination," offered a literary method. Thinking by analogy—by "correspondences"—was what, to replace the discursive tedium of the scientists and George Eliot, Yeats needed. Thrice-great Hermes, upholding imagination in defiance of fact, made him a symbolist.

A symbol, for Yeats, was any thing of words or any concrete object that by correspondence with Anima Mundi, the Platonic memory up there, causes an influence to descend down here: "As above, so below," great Hermes said. The magical correspondence, working like a push button, causes a definite response; but response to the literary correspondence is at once certain and indefinite. As magus, Yeats employed the one to cure fevers; as poet, he was almost content with writing poems. The essays "Magic" (1901) and "The Symbolism of Poetry" (1900) make his intentions plain. In "Magic," where magus and poet are rival enchanters, he tells how the "great memory can be evoked by symbols." In the earlier essay, he deals with literary evocation, the "indefinable symbolism which is the substance of all style." Now the symbol is any suggestive embodiment—word, rhythm, image, or poem—any "musical relation" of parts that has "new meaning every day."

His poems of the 1890s are filled with occult matters, "the Ineffable Name," for example, and Mme. Blavatsky's elementals. But references are not necessarily symbols. The best examples of symbolism are the poems Yeats wrote about the rose, emblem of the Rosicrucians and of the great work of alchemy. A natural shape that suggests unity, a rose brings many traditional blooms to mind: Dante's rose, the dark rose of Ireland, and the dozen roses one gives to a girl on occasion. "The Secret Rose," including these customary meanings and, apparently, uniting nation, love, and the occult, is secret nevertheless—not only remote but unknown and unknowable. Not multiple meanings but ultimate secrecy and the question mark that ends the poem guarantee symbol.

The occult combatants of "The Rose of Battle" are "insatiable" and sad because, never getting to the bottom of what they evoke, they confront unanswerable questions. As for the "rosy peace" between contending opposites that Yeats hopefully celebrates in "The Rose of Peace," this peace proved to be no more than armistice. He began to feel lost on a road that changed and shifted as he walked, a road that, as innocent of Greek as of Latin, he liked to call "Hodos Chameliontos."

Less road than maze: "I plunged without clue into a laby-
rinth of . . . 'unintelligible images' "—images that fresh
images begot. It is easy to laugh at Yeats's attempt upon Anima
Mundi, but to laugh at this Hermetic affair is, after all, to
laugh at Plato, and the prudent man would rather laugh at
someone else.

Getting lost was only one of the crosses awaiting those who
"pulled the Immortal Rose." Exile from love and nation seemed
the lot of those who pulled too hard. Yeats's Fergus, giving
up nation to become a druid, must also give up love. Yeats's
wandering Aengus, the Irish equivalent of Hermes, pursues in
vain the woman he has conjured up. His desire to pluck
golden apples with one hand and silver apples with the other
in a kind of Eden is a desire for an impossible union of imagination and fact. These heroes dramatically project the poet's
trouble; but Yeats also spoke of it directly—in, for example,
"To the Rose upon the Rood of Time," a Rosicrucian en-
counter of eternity with time, imagination with fact. "Come
near," Yeats implores the rose, but not too near—not so near
that, swallowed up by rosiness, he be kept from "common
things" and the affairs of Eire. The dangers of the rose are
her monopoly and his loneliness; promising unity, she divides.
Fear of this division also fills "To Ireland in the Coming
Times":

> Nor may I less be counted one
> With Davis, Mangan, Ferguson,
> Because . . .

Because, surrounded by "elemental creatures" that come from
"unmeasured mind," Yeats cannot take his eyes from "the
red-rose-bordered hem." She who trails it, no mortal girl, is
a girl to distract druids alone. "Rosa Alchemica" (1896) is
the most elaborate account of the problem. In this short story,
that owes splendor to the decors of Pater, Villiers de l'Isle-

Adam, and the pre-Raphaelites, Michael Robartes (the occult side of Yeats) invites the aesthetic narrator (the more worldly side of Yeats) to a Rosicrucian ceremony, where, in a chamber with rose on ceiling, cross on floor, adepts dance with spirits until the peasants of the vicinity raid the place. Disenchantment follows too much enchantment. The terrified narrator, abandoning apartness, both aesthetic and occult, relapses into reality.

But reality could not detain young Yeats for long. When it proved too much for him, he fled it, in fancy, to islands, sometimes with an imaginary girl, sometimes without, and, later, to hair tents which, however real, kept reality out. That his poems of escape are, on the whole, his best of the 1880s and 1890s proves that his heart was in them and all the power of his fancy.

"The Indian to His Love," recalling Spenser, is a vision of an island of tranquillity, with peahens dancing on smooth lawns, and the cooing of Tennyson's "burnished dove" to remind the poet and his dream girl "how far away are the unquiet lands." Yet even here these lotus eaters miss complete tranquillity and order; for the raging of an intrusive parrot reminds them of what they have all but forgotten. Oisin, too, has his reminders. His escape from the affairs of Ireland on a fairy horse spurred westward by Niamh, a girl of the Sidhe, to the Land of Youth is satisfactory until a spear floating by this island of irresponsibility recalls the claims of heroic discipline and the troubles of adults. These escapers are reminded or called back. Not so the escaper to Innisfree, a bushy little island in Lough Gill, near Sligo; for, actually on the pavement of Piccadilly, he only dreams of arising and going now.

"Who Goes with Fergus?" the best poem of his prentice years, is one of the best of our time. Why else would Joyce's Buck Mulligan sing it to Stephen Dedalus on their tower, and why else would Stephen, brooding on mother, brood on it?

Not only a poem of escape to "a woven world-forgotten isle," as Yeats puts it in "The Man Who Dreamed of Faeryland," this is a poem of retreat to infancy, the Land of Youth again, where, with mother and father in charge, love is no longer a bother.

William Empson found this poem an ambiguous thing—of the seventh type perhaps, a type that, by saying nothing, allows the reader, projecting what he pleases, to say all. Is the opening line, for example, invitation or warning? And what about "now"? Empson asks, forgetting that now is a word that Irishmen like to end questions with. But much of the poem is plain enough: imagery of piercing, driving, and ruling seems paternal; the woods and "the white breast of the dim sea" are as clearly maternal. It is clear that Fergus, driving his brazen car, like a sun god, is still a man of affairs and that, ruling the shadows of the wood, the sea, and the comets, he has druid powers. Being with a man of this capacity, a benign papa who allows sporting on the green, makes one a child again. "Woven," the key word, implies a union here of disparate things unlikely in the world out there. Less ambiguous than it seems at first, the poem is an invitation to get away— especially from troubles with girls like Maud Gonne. But Empson is right in holding that what the reader is forced to project is the heart of the poem. Unlimited by the particulars of retreat, the poem becomes a form for a variety of feelings and their symbol: first a question, then a double chiasmus ("Young man . . . maid," "brood . . . brood"), then a triumph ("brazen cars"), and last a peaceful decline assured, yet slowed, by those excellent spondees. If "dishevelled" hints less than complete order and security, something unwoven, the hint is no more than a reminder of conditions off island; and, what is more, "dishevelled" implies hair, the material for tents.

Better than islands, hair tents are what you enjoy when

your girl, lying on top of you, lets her long hair down around your head. Yeats's islands were dreams; not so his hair tents. The girl in question was not Maud Gonne but another, more accommodating—and hairier perhaps. "He Bids His Beloved Be at Peace," hairiest of the hairy poems, opens with a vision of horses, terribly maned. Such things outdoors demand refuge indoors:

> Beloved, let your eyes half close, and your heart beat
> Over my heart, and your hair fall over my breast.

Agreeable "twilight" keeps hair of a different color out of sight. Agreeable too the veil in *Axël*, a play by Villiers de l'Isle-Adam that, along with *Prometheus Unbound*, Yeats counted among his "sacred books." Not only the Rosicrucian theme and a castle made *Axël* irresistible, but enclosure of a cozier sort: "O to veil you with my hair where you will breathe the spirit of dead roses."

Emerging from his tent at last, Yeats went to Dublin in 1899, with George Moore and Edward Martyn, to establish, for the improvement of the Irish, a literary theater. At the first performance of *The Countess Cathleen*, a "tapestry" of verse, the unimproved Irish rioted—all but Stephen Dedalus.

To replace the discarded "truth" of "Oisin," *Cathleen* offered what Yeats was to call a "counter-truth." Far from insular, this play approaches the world, which, as Yeats had come to think, was divided into three kinds: aristocrats, peasants, and merchants. The aristocrat in *Cathleen*, at once heroic and public-spirited, saves the peasants from the designs of the merchants. Nothing to cause a riot in this folk tale save a theological irregularity that Yeats, trying to elevate and unite a country he did not understand, had been careless of. The soft and dreamy verse of *Cathleen*, more important to Yeats than the plot, was meant to enchant the Irish as it enchanted its maker. For him, as yet, the stage was no more than a place to hear his verses spoken on. Moore came upon the poet, during rehearsal one day, teaching the actors how to chant: "One can hear that kind of thing, my dear fellow," said Moore, "on Sunday, in any Methodist chapel."

The verse of *Cathleen*, "Oisin," and most of the early lyrics is, as Yeats himself said later on, "vague and sentimental." A hatred of abstraction and of Victorian rhetoric, he said, had driven him to their opposite. But whatever his distaste for abstraction, he had not discovered concretion—even as late as 1898 when, in "The Autumn of the Body," he said that his thoughts were filled "with the essences of things, and not with things." "Dim" and "glimmering," closer to essence than to thing maybe, were favorite words, together with "dove-grey" and "pearl-pale," which on June 16, 1904, inspired Buck Mulligan's "new art colour for our Irish poets: snotgreen." The rhythms, composed by ear for the ear without knowledge of metrics, suited the diction. But there are occasional triumphs of rhythm, in "The Sad Shepherd," for example, or "The Rose of Peace." "To Some I Have Talked with by the Fire," approaching the sweep of Milton, catches something of his grandeur. Surely Yeats was a man for whom words alone were certain good; but had he died in 1900 or thereabouts, with most of his fellow Rhymers, he would be classed with them today as a minor poet of the decadence. He had not found a style. "In those great ignorant leafy ways," a line from "The Two Trees," may seem an anticipation of the style that, after facing the world, he was to find; but this line, written years later to replace the soft original, is that style itself.

The second period, bringing style, began in 1902 with three poems: "The Folly of Being Comforted," "Adam's Curse," and "The Players Ask for a Blessing on the Psalteries." In the first of these the rhythm, diction, and tone are those, at first, of ordinary conversation, elevated a little by the tight frame of couplets. "Time" may be abstract, but time's effects, gray hair and shadows about the eyes, are what we discover day by day. Out of the quotidian, however, comes sudden glory: "The fire that stirs about her, when she stirs." Charged with anguished ambiguity, the last couplet takes on the "great nobleness" Yeats saw in Maud Gonne. "Adam's Curse" is also a conversation, with Maud and another this time and this time about laboring. The image of a moon worn out by laboring may be a vestige—perhaps an intentional echo of, or farewell to, early Yeats; but the rest of the poem is in the new manner: natural words in the natural order. Lines which must seem "a moment's thought" have taken hours "maybe." The word "maybe," marking the discovery of a new region, is the concentrate and the triumph of this poem. These two poems, unlike those of the 1890s, are written in what Yeats called "living speech," not that of Galway peasants or of journalists, but what is spoken by those who speak best, selected and heightened. "I tried," said Yeats, "to make the language of poetry that of passionate normal speech." Normal speech maybe, but there is nothing common or mean about "maybe" in its setting.

"The Players Ask for a Blessing on the Psalteries" is an extravagant little play with characters, action, suspense, climax, and, divided voices becoming one, the spending of all passions —a little play, yet not unlike "Alexander's Feast" in character and matter. Gaiety that brings angels down cannot abate the seriousness of a traditional theme: art is long, life, fleeting. The art of the players, at once "proud and careless," is the art of these three new poems. As "maybe" is the key to "Adam's Curse," so "glittering," replacing "glimmering" and marking the extent of the change that had come upon the poet, is the key to this. The psaltery, an instrument acquired in the glimmering period, is a kind of zither on which Yeats liked to accompany the chanting of his verses. (Tone-deaf, he found "quarter-tones" best for this purpose.) But psalteries in the hands of these players have lost their original air. The lyric, distanced now and impersonal, has become dramatic.

The cause of this great, sudden change invites conjecture. Bitterness over Maud Gonne? She married MacBride in 1903, a year too late, but the preparation of her "crazy salad" may have dismayed Yeats and hardened him. Disenchantment with Ireland? Offering fine words to "a mob that knows neither literature nor art" was surely discouraging. Experience in the theater? Putting plays on could have turned his thoughts to speech.

From 1903 to 1917 Yeats managed the Abbey Theatre, wrote heroic plays in scorn of his audience, and spent the summers at Coole under the care of Lady Gregory. As champion of Synge, his discovery and his friend, Yeats faced the hostile pit, fielded the dead cats, and intrepidly threw them back. Learning that plays are not lyrics, he designed poetic plays as plays, *On Baile's Strand* (1904) among them—one of several on Cuchulain's death. Home from the theater or from Coole, he tried to create his "permanent self" by collecting his essays, poems, and plays. To assure the "organic wholeness" of his image he revised his early poems and even the letters he had kept copies of. He wrote so little poetry from 1903 to 1912 that we cannot blame George Moore for thinking Yeats, like other poets of the 1890s, was through: a manager maybe, a collector and reviser of old work, a feudal retainer of Lady Gregory, and a writer of unacceptable plays, but a poet no more.

The poems Yeats did write during this time, most of them included in *The Green Helmet* (1910), continue and improve the new manner of 1902. Still conversational in rhythm and

[15]

word, these poems are more sinewy and, as he said, more "masculine" than their predecessors. Good-by to his ignoble past in a "dim shadowy region" of "disembodied beauty": "Now I may wither into the truth." Withering brought "lofty severity," he thought, and with it "hard energy," "intensity," "ecstasy," "discipline." A craftsman now, he was just in these estimates of a craft "clear and straightforward . . . strong and simple." Taking his embroidered coat off, he had discovered "enterprise in walking naked." No more decorations, no more abstractions, no more "rhetoric," but things coldly and precisely rendered—less often in images now than in great, bare statements: "My barren thoughts have chilled me to the bone." As for themes: Maud Gonne, now confused with Helen of Troy, still bothered him. And sometimes he wrote about the troubles of the day:

> . . . My curse on plays
> That have to be set up in fifty ways,
> On the day's war with every knave and dolt. . . .

But the characteristic verses of this time are satiric epigrams, occasional in theme and classical in deportment: "On Hearing That the Students of Our New University Have Joined the Agitation Against Immoral Literature" or "On Those That Hated 'The Playboy of the Western World,' 1907." The dogs, fleas, and eunuchs of these bitter things would not have pleased young Yeats. Instead of Shelley now, or Morris, he turned for models to Landor, Ben Jonson, and Chaucer. (An influence is what a man is ready for.) In 1912 he discovered John Donne, whose masculine line, the speech "of a man thinking and feeling," seemed—long before Eliot said so—what a poet needs these days.

The influence of Ezra Pound is less certain. He came to visit Yeats in 1909 and from 1912 to 1916 served, on and off, as his secretary. In 1909 Pound was still imitating the poems of young Yeats, those of *The Wind among the Reeds* (1899) in particular. Yeats, who had turned his back on these, had been writing poetry in his new manner for seven years, and for seven years, in letters and essays, had been commending what Pound was to commend: brevity, intensity, concreteness; had been condemning what Pound was to condemn: abstraction, rhetoric, and inversion. It is likely that Pound learned of these things from Yeats, abetted perhaps by T. E. Hulme. Having learned them, Pound vigorously taught the master what he had taught. Accepting the lessons, Yeats was pleased when, after correcting his poems, Pound sent them off to magazines. It is a fact that in 1912 Yeats, enjoying a revival of energy, began to write more and better poems than he had written for years. Pound's effect on these, if any, may have been the excitement of his presence; or, perhaps, more than trigger, Pound may have confirmed Yeats in his established ways. Anyway, it is clear that interaction of one sort or another accounts for much in the work of both poets. Later, after they had drifted apart, Pound dismissed some of Yeats's greatest poems with a single word: "putrid." Yeats contented himself with calling Pound a poet "not of my school."

But Pound's effect on Yeats's plays is plain. Enlightened by Ernest Fenollosa, Pound told Yeats about the Noh plays of Japan, a form he found "distinguished, indirect, and symbolic . . . an aristocratic form," independent of mob or press when presented with "august formality," to the accompaniment of gong and drum, in some great lady's drawing room. Such a play, "playing upon a single metaphor," was the "image of nobility" Yeats had been looking for, something with all the "severe appropriate beauty," all the discipline and high breeding that tradition confers. Here was ceremony itself, here the "distance from reality" that one esteems who has looked at reality too long. *At the Hawk's Well*, the first of four Noh plays Yeats wrote, was presented in 1916 in Lady Cunard's drawing room. Though *The Only Jealousy of Emer* (1919) is the best of the four, "A woman's beauty," the poem sung at the unfolding of the curtain, is a poem so beautiful that the play seems little more than its occasion and its setting:

> A woman's beauty is like a white
> Frail bird, like a white sea-bird alone
> At daybreak after stormy night
> Between two furrows upon the ploughed land:
> A sudden storm, and it was thrown
> Between dark furrows upon the ploughed land.
> How many centuries spent
> The sedentary soul
> In toils of measurement
> Beyond eagle or mole,
> Beyond hearing or seeing,
> Or Archimedes' guess,
> To raise into being
> That loveliness?

Not Noh, however aristocratic, but Lady Gregory herself gave Yeats his experience of aristocracy. Her "feudal sense of responsibility" saved him from journalism by timely hand-outs while, at Coole, she showed him the spacious life. More than this, she put Castiglione's *Book of the Courtier* into his hands to enlarge his vision of the good, high life. Taking him, so entranced, to Italy, she pointed to Urbino, the place of Castiglione and his courtiers, long ago, in a time unlike our democratic time. In place and book Yeats found the ideal of the renaissance great man, whose courtly "nonchalance," transposed, became the artist's "nonchalance of the hand." The craft of seeming without craft, praised as early as "Adam's Curse," and the other lessons of Castiglione account for the demeanor of what Yeats began to write in 1912.

"To a Wealthy Man Who Promised a Second Subscription to the Dublin Municipal Gallery If It Were Proved the People Wanted Pictures" (1912), a poem written on the occasion of

Hugh Lane's difficulties with the middle class, is the plainest reflection of Castiglione. (Lane, a collector of paintings, was Lady Gregory's nephew.) The wealthy man wants halfpennies from the mob as evidence of interest before he will put his guineas down—as if

> . . . things it were a pride to give
> Are what the blind and ignorant town
> Imagines best to make it thrive.

Aristocrats at Ferrara and Urbino were careless of public approval. What cared Duke Ercole for the "onion-sellers" or

> . . . Guidobaldo, when he made
> That grammar school of courtesies
> Where wit and beauty learned their trade
> Upon Urbino's windy hill,

and what cared Cosimo when he established a great library?

> Whence turbulent Italy should draw
> Delight in Art whose end is peace,
> In logic and in natural law
> By sucking at the dugs of Greece.

Aside from tone and feeling, the remarkable thing about this poem is the management of prosaic and logical syntax within a metric frame. No longer avoided but used, abstractions make neighboring particulars stand out as particulars restore life to their neighbors.

The good dukes of Ferrara and Urbino took their place in the hierarchy with Cuchulain, who now seemed less hero than aristocrat. To embody his feelings about these superior men Yeats invented two figures, the fisherman and the horseman. Disenchantment with the ordinary men of Ireland charges the three troubled beats of "The Fisherman" until the magnificent ending:

> Maybe a twelvemonth since
> Suddenly I began,
> In scorn of this audience,
> Imagining a man
>
> . . .

Climbing up to a place
Where stone is dark under froth,
And the down-turn of his wrist
When the flies drop in the stream;
A man who does not exist,
A man who is but a dream;
And cried, 'Before I am old
I shall have written him one
Poem maybe as cold
And passionate as the dawn.'

This aristocratic fisherman is also the poet, master of a cold
and passionate craft, and his impossible audience. Not even
the fisherman, however, was safe from contamination by Ireland; for Yeats was to see

. . . a likely lad
That had a sound fly-fisher's wrist
Turn to a drunken journalist.

The elegy for Major Robert Gregory, Lady Gregory's son,
presents the horseman, the rider to hounds; but more than
rider, skilled in all high pursuits, Gregory was "Our Sidney
and our perfect man." Castiglione's courtier in the flesh, such
a man should be above "that discourtesy of death":

Soldier, scholar, horseman, he,
And all he did done perfectly
As though he had but that one trade alone.

Yeats was exploring again the apparent incompatibility of conversational ease within the limits of an intricate stanza (this
one taken from Abraham Cowley) that seems to forbid all
easiness. The dignity of the form elevates, as it limits, the in-
timacy of a man talking to his peers around the fire.

The folly, they say, of a man who, in these middle-class
times, set his heart on a kind of dignity that had vanished from
the world—except for some vestiges at Coole and other great
houses not yet torn down or burned. How, they ask, can a
poet of our time turn his back on it and write its appropriate

song? But, far from turning his back, Yeats faced what he abhorred. And his poems owe their grandeur, the air of casual, strict nobility, to the very thing they question. Less folly here perhaps than a craftsman's necessity. A cold and passionate grandeur may have been what Yeats needed to keep his own disorder down. But before we accost his "mask," more great poems of 1912 and the following years attend us.

"To a Shade" (1913) concerns Hugh Lane and Parnell, both rejected by Ireland. Irony, foreign to early Yeats but not to our time, provides the devastating parenthesis: "(I wonder if the builder has been paid)." "For they are at their old tricks yet" is cliché transfigured. Elevated by such common means, the poem, like those "gaunt houses," puts on a majesty that the final dissonance of "come" and "tomb" serves only to improve.

Since "Adam's Curse" Yeats had seen the virtue of dissonant or imperfect rhymes. After the displeasures of 1912 and 1913 he began to use them with liberal hand—as, for example, in "The Scholars," where "despair" and "ear" leave us dissatisfied until the appeasement of "say" and "way." Like young Mozart, who got out of bed to resolve a discord struck on the piano by his father, Yeats commonly resolved his discords in the end by rhyme. But, serving their turn, the discords had expressed his bitterness. The final concord is a reminder of things as they ought to be.

The bitterness of "September 1913" was occasioned by fumblers "in a greasy till" who, provoked by a strike on the docks, had locked the workers out. The middle class had killed the "romantic Ireland" of John O'Leary, Robert Emmet, and all the "wild geese," those Irishmen who, fleeing to France after the Boyne, had transferred their energies to the making of Hennessey and the noble wine of Haut-Brion—French for O'Brien. This poem, relying on more than dissonance, irony, and revitalized cliché, owes its triumph to a firm structure of question and qualification and to the dramatic contrast of plain talk with grand refrain. That the heart of the poet was not altogether given to the heroes he praised is suggested by the ambiguity of "delirium" and "maddened."

Neither rebel nor wild goose—though an admirer, at a distance, of both—Yeats shows himself again in a companion piece, "Easter 1916," on the rising against the English. Spring with all its hope has repaired the decay of September—more or less; for Yeats's admiration is qualified by fear of bewildering "excess," the un-Irish thought that England "may keep faith," and the puzzling transfiguration of men and women into heroes. Patrick Pearse, the leader of the insurrection, was a bad poet, as the irony of "our wingèd horse" makes evident. That "vainglorious lout," John MacBride, had married Maud Gonne. Con Markiewicz, though once a rider to hounds, had become shrill in argument. From such as these and from the "casual comedy" of Dublin only a "terrible," plainly ambiguous, beauty could be born. The great, spare poem, less about the rising than about the poet's mixed response, is a poem of thought in process—a poem of a man thinking second thoughts.

There is nothing casual about the comedy of "The Three Hermits":

> First was muttering a prayer,
> Second rummaged for a flea;
> On a windy stone, the third,
> Giddy with his hundredth year,
> Sang unnoticed like a bird.

Grotesque comedy, at odds with grandeur, is a product of the "mask," and grandeur is another.

Yeats accounted to himself for the great change of 1902 by his theory of the mask. The idea of putting a mask on, perhaps from Oscar Wilde, came to Yeats in the late 1890s. But the theory he needed to account for what he had been doing did not develop fully until "Ego Dominus Tuus" (1915), more play than poem. Hic and Ille—plainly ancient Romans—are the dramatis personae. Hic (or this one here), the subjective, personal side of the artist, wants to find and express himself. Ille (or that one there), the objective, impersonal side, summons his opposite by an "image" or mask. Dante, says Ille, gained "nonchalance of the hand" by expressing, through a mask, his "anti-self."

Putting a mask on, then, is writing as if you were someone else—and for many this would be a help. Plainly you cannot be someone else; but if you think you are, you may suppress one side of your nature and enlarge another, potentially there but neglected until now. Since a *persona*, or mask, is something you speak through, what you say, changed by its passage through a hole in another's face, is another's yet your own. The wearer of a *persona* can be personal and impersonal at once, subjective and objective. At a distance from his matter, he can shape it.

Yeats, having come to think himself sentimental, feared that self-expression would produce more soft and glimmering poems. But if he became his opposite, his verse would take on hardness and glitter. Through the mask of his opposite, he achieved the dramatic impersonality commended by Stephen Dedalus and, after him, by T. S. Eliot. No less personal than before he put the mask on, Yeats became to all appearances impersonal, at once involved with his affairs and so distant from them that he could display a courtier's nonchalance and the nonchalance of the artist. Balancing opposites, his mask brought unity—to the work.

In "The Collar-Bone of a Hare" Yeats goes to another island, not for escape this time but for distant scrutiny of the shore he has left. Drilling a hole through the bone, he stares at things on shore as if through a monocle. Staring through a bone is equivalent, in a way, to sounding through a mask.

If this poem is about the mask, "The Saint and the Hunchback" is the mask's product. Here, speaking of his own concerns, Yeats is not himself at all; staging his conflicts in a little comedy, he makes the work resolve them. Saint and Hunchback, the contenders, represent two sides of the poet. All they have in common is the image of Alcibiades, a Greek anticipation of Castiglione's courtier. "That great rogue Alcibiades," within both speakers yet distant from both, brings unity. So too a little drama of technique: troubled rhythms and the dissonance of "thrash" and "flesh" find concord in the smoothness of the final couplet and its final rhyme of "degrees" with "Alcibiades." "That," the important word, recalls Ille and predicts "Sailing to Byzantium." Through his distancing mask Yeats became the poet of thatness—as Hopkins, by other devices, the poet of thisness. But thatness and this poem belong to the third period.

The third period—much overlapping here and no clear edges—begins in 1918 perhaps. Poems of this period, improving the developments of the second, take another and a loftier character from new matter: the tower, the wheeling moon, and the trouble of growing old. Yeats and Wordsworth are alike in respect of this: both developed. As Wordsworth got worse and worse, so Yeats got better and better. By agreement among men of taste and judgment the later poems of Yeats—those in *The Tower* (1928), for example—are best.

In 1917, having been rejected by Iseult Gonne, Maud's daughter, Yeats married George Hyde-Lees. In 1918, he brought his wife to the tall, square tower (not far from Coole) that a lecture tour in the States had provided the money for. In this damp, romantic retreat, he endured the political and military troubles of 1919 and 1922. When they made him a senator in 1923, he moved to Dublin. Receiving the Nobel Prize that same year, he thought the court of Sweden next best to that of Urbino.

"To Be Carved on a Stone at Thoor Ballylee" is the first of many poems the tower inspired. Beginning grandly with "I, the poet William Yeats, " the inscription—still there on the wall—proceeds ambiguously to "my wife George." (Is the omission of a comma after "wife" intentional or not?) Yeats found the tower a ruin, and, foreseeing ruin again, had it repaired—less as residence perhaps than as symbol: "I declare this tower is my symbol." The ruinous top suggested our times and what he thought his own dilapidation; but the tower also embodied tradition and nobility. Surely some aristocrat, even of the second class, built it; and Swift, had he been in the vicinity, could have climbed the winding stair—Burke and Berkeley too, had they been that way inclined. ("Blood and the Moon" deals with these possibilities.) The towers of literature are places, sometimes, for the solitary pursuit of wisdom. It pleased Yeats to think of Milton's Hermetic student, his lamp burning at midnight "in som high lonely Towr" or of Shelley's studious Prince Athanase, "apart from men, as in a lonely tower." Lamp and tower became images for Yeats "of mysterious wisdom won by toil." A castle-keep in bad times, a shelter against the "roof-levelling wind," an observatory with a moderate prospect—all these meanings and more, crowding the image, explain the fascination it held for the poet.

The tower is shelter and a reminder of gentleness in "A Prayer for my Daughter" (1919). With more than a father's common anxiety, Yeats prays that this girl, safe as yet in her crib in the tower, never go the way of Maud Gonne or of Venus, whose crazy-salad days are not exemplary. May this girl, schooled by Castiglione, follow what is customary, ceremonious. Wind (sometimes from the sea, sometimes from Vulcan's bellows) and shelter are the contending images: the "murderous innocence" of unlimited nature and the "radical innocence" of a tree of birds in a garden with walls. This accurate structure belongs with three meditations, also centered in the tower: "Nineteen Hundred and Nineteen" (1919), "Meditations in Time of Civil War" (1923), and "The Tower" (1925), sequences, composed in a variety of measures, that seem one long poem on the violence of the times and the destruction of all "ingenious lovely things." Man thinking modern thoughts determines the words, their rhythm, and the arrangement of parts; great man thinking ancient thoughts determines the nobility of tone: "Come let us mock at the great. . . ."

In "The Tower" the meditator turns from the times to time itself—to old age that, now that ear and eye are failing, has condemned him to abstraction and argument. Age has tied "a sort of battered kettle at the heel." Self-examination, memories, and the prospect from the tower lead to a testament in the manner of Villon: leaving his pride to fishermen, Yeats declares his faith in man's power to make. In these three poems Cowley's stanza often contends with the rhythm of speech "to elevate a rhyme"—a purpose served by ottava rima in two later but related poems on the great house and the tower, Coole Park and Ballylee. Meditation, upon a swallow's flight at first, brings the poet at last to high horses, now riderless, in the darkening estates. Lovers of high estate,

> We were the last romantics—chose for theme
> Traditional sanctity and loveliness.

His wife, George, brought wisdom, humor, and balance to that tower if "Michael Robartes and the Dancer" and "Solomon and the Witch" may be relied on. "Great Solomon," teased by his Sheba, has learned to tease himself. The very wife he needed, George kept him amused. She began, shortly after their marriage, to mutter in bed at night, every night, what seemed fragments of a doctrine dictated by daemons. She also took to automatic writing. Her distracted husband, putting Iseult off and the fragments together, stayed in bed or near it, busy. His construction, announced in "The Phases of the Moon," is displayed in *A Vision*—in the limited edition of 1925 and in the rewritten version of 1937, the one in print now. Sometimes the second version, reworking the first, makes it less immoderate: the *Speculum* . . . *Hominorum* (a sixteenth-century folio) of 1925 becomes the *Speculum* . . . *Hominum* of 1937. Giraldus, the author of one or the other of these folios, looks, in the sixteenth-century woodcut that embellishes both texts, like Yeats.

Yeats had the phases of the moon—what he called the "Great Wheel"—in mind when he wrote most of his poems of the 1920s; but, reading these, we need know little about phase or wheel. Indeed, a little seems too much, his business none of ours. There are, to be sure, a few intrusions: "perne in a gyre" is either the one defect of "Sailing to Byzantium" or else a kind of beauty spot. "The Double Vision of Michael Robartes," requiring knowledge of the system, remains a private poem. But "The Saint and the Hunchback" can be read without knowing this:

In a month, the moon, circling the earth, proceeds through twenty-eight phases: the full, the dark, and twenty-six with more or less of light and dark. An unbroken circle and the balancing of opposites combine the unity Yeats desired with the change he was condemned to. Let light be spirit, imagination, and all that is subjective. Let dark be matter, fact—the objective. Then the full moon, phase 15, is Anima Mundi or Plato's heaven; the dark moon, phase 1, is a hell of matter. Phases 1 and 15, being unmixed, are out of time; but the other phases, changing in time, permit life. In this cyclical balancing of timelessness and time, spirit and matter, subjective and objective, imagination and fact, Yeats found the symbol of all he had to know of psychology, history, and aesthetics. Psychological types, determined by proportion of light and dark, proceed by metempsychosis from the butcher of phase 2, through the hero of phase 12, to the hunchback, saint, and fool of the last three phases. History proceeds in cycles of two thousand years from a dark age, through an age of enlightenment, to decline and fall into darkness again. For his aesthetics Yeats combined wheel and mask: a man in the lighter phases must balance himself by the mask of his opposite in the dark half of the circle of necessity. The masked poet may write like a fool; the masked statesman speaks like a butcher. Less like a wheel than a bedspring, the whole affair is a gyre.

This lunar system, propounded in *A Vision*, was an excitement and a comfort. Excited, as in 1912 by Pound, Yeats hurried to his table, there to write poems he thought greater than his earlier poems in "self-possession and power." As for comfort—a better word here than belief: "My critical mind . . . mocked, and yet I was delighted"—the system, doing for him what the Church did for Joyce, provided an ordering frame. From this a world of image and reference: "We have come," said those daemons, "to give you metaphors for poetry." And, sending Yeats to the library, the system made an educated man of him, a man able and eager to find parallel or example in history, literature, and myth. A private system made him a public poet.

Each gyre of history, unwinding for two thousand years, begins with a conjunction of girl and bird, of Mary and the Pigeon for our cycle, of Leda and the Swan for the cycle before ours. Part of a private system maybe, the Swan, Leda, and the two eggs she laid are common knowledge—so too are Helen and Clytemnestra, who, hatched from those two eggs, caused all the trouble at Troy and Agamemnon's death. (A third egg that some talk about seems fabulous.) No sonnet more public, then, than "Leda and the Swan" (1923), and few so grand. From divine intercourse—"feathered glory" above and "loosening thighs" below—we descend to consequences of "burning roof and tower" and to a third unanswerable question, this one epistemological. "Indifferent beak" or the other particulars of loving, elegance of phrase or syntax, unanswerable questions—in which does the glory of this poem lie?

"Two Songs from a Play" is about the beginning of Mary's cycle and the end of Leda's. "Fabulous darkness" and "Babylonian starlight" refer to phase 1 or the dark of the moon. Such privacies become public by the aid of Plato, Frazer's *Golden Bough*, and Vergil. Dionysus, one of Frazer's dying and rising gods, represents the old order. The fierce "staring virgin" who presides ritually at his death is both the Virgin Mary, who, with Pigeon's blood, started the new order, and Astraea or Virgo, associated with the golden age. "Magnus Annus," a public gyre, is Plato's great year, which, now in early spring, promises more of the same:

> Another Troy must rise and set,
> Another lineage feed the crow,
> Another Argo's painted prow
> Drive to a flashier bauble yet.

(The golden fleece of the new cycle will be "flashier" because each cycle is a little less estimable than its predecessor. Castor and Pollux, two of the Argonauts, were hatched from Leda's eggs.) For these lines public-spirited Yeats drew upon an old tradition. Vergil, praising renewal in his fourth, or "Messianic," eclogue, was the first to speak of another Argo and another Troy. Dryden, in "Alexander's Feast," echoes Vergil; then Shelley, echoing Vergil and Dryden, watered them down for the chorus in *Hellas:*

> The world's great age begins anew,
>   The golden years return,
>
>   . . .
>
> A loftier Argo cleaves the main,
>   Fraught with a later prize;
> Another Orpheus sings again,
>   And loves, and weeps, and dies.
>
>   . . .

> Another Athens shall arise,
> And to remoter time
> Bequeath, like sunset to the skies,
> The splendour of its prime.

Yeats knew Vergil's eclogue; and Shelley, who sounds in these lines like early Yeats, was early Yeats's favorite. A comparison of Shelley's looseness—all those stale words and phrases—with the tightness, brilliance, and finality of Yeats shows the difference between a barefaced poet and one with a mask on—or, maybe, between poets of the second class and the first.

"Staring" and "And" in dreamlike sequence establish, as "Two Songs from a Play" begins, an atmosphere of trance and disorder at odds with the rational neatness of the stanza. The question behind the poem, says Yeats, is that of the rational man: "What if the irrational should return?" Here, the civilization of Greece yields to darkness, ritual violence, and "Galilean turbulence":

> Odour of blood when Christ was slain
> Made all Platonic tolerance vain
> And vain all Doric discipline.

These climactic lines may owe some of their radiance to the collocation of the abstract and the concrete or to the nostalgic chiasmus of "vain"; but that such arrangements evade the critical eye is suggested by the first version:

> Made Plato's tolerance in vain
> And vain the Doric discipline.

These words and their order, though almost the same, lack magic. In his *Autobiography* Yeats finds all the difference in the world between "particular bright star" and "bright particular star."

The last stanza of "Two Songs," not there when these songs brought the curtain up and down in *The Resurrection*, is a commendable afterthought; for the intensity of the penultimate stanza demands relaxation. Nothing more appropriate for its place than this declining coda.

As "The Lake Isle of Innisfree" is esteemed as a vision of escape, so "The Second Coming," as a vision of our world. Toward all of us—indifferent best and passionate worst alike—a monstrous threat comes slouching. But Castiglione's "ceremony of innocence" also stirs the bourgeois heart. However aristocratic, the falcon and his falconer make gyres public property; and the echo of Donne's "Anniversary" brings literary tradition to bear. Yet in their private capacities the beast and the sphinx, more than vaguely menacing, embody two cycles—the one before ours, the other, after. The first coming was that of Jesus, whose "rocking cradle" vexed the sphinx. Another Bethlehem will replace the Virgin's and another second-comer, her Son. Maybe this "rough beast" is also a second sphinx; but our knowledge of such matters is questioned at the end.

The irregular verse is not—and was not meant to be—free verse, that "joyless" rhythm of "modern poets" which, said Yeats, is too "personal and original" for him: "I must choose a traditional stanza." He was not altogether unacquainted with the modern poets who displeased him. In 1924 he said: "The other day . . . I read that strange 'Waste Land' by Mr. T. C. Eliot."

Occupying phase 15 of a temporal cycle, Yeats's Byzantium is at once in time and out of it, less an actual city, therefore, than a "holy city" or, at least, the half of one. His idea of this city was a long time growing. In 1907, when Lady Gregory showed Yeats the mosaics at Ravenna, Byzantium, encountered there, became for him a place of art: mosaics, domes, and goldsmith's work. He read books, in one of which he found Justinian and in another the mechanical golden bird of the Emperor Theophilus. When Yeats put his system together, his idea of Byzantium seemed a suitable climax (or fifteenth phase) for the Christian cycle. More or less out of time, the city became a refuge from time and, at once purgatory and paradise, a haunt of spirits. As for place: happily situated at the junction of East and West, uniting these opposites, the city would do as a symbol of "unity of being." Going there became the process of unifying. Enjoying a "unity of culture" impossible today, the city could serve as a center, before Castiglione's Urbino, for lords and ladies. As the fifteenth phase, Byzantium, becoming an image of Anima Mundi or Plato's store of ideas, acquired literary significance. Of the two poems Yeats wrote about this compendious spot, "Sailing to Byzantium" (1927) and "Byzantium" (1930), the second is more faithful to his ideas of the city, but the first is a better poem.

The speaker of "Sailing to Byzantium" is an old man who, surrounded by young lovers and sick with desire, would be easier somewhere else, dead maybe. That the speaker is Yeats, the poet of thatness, is established by the first word, "That"; and "That," implying attitude toward and distance from, proves that, leaving the young to "one another's arms," he has crossed those "mackerel-crowded seas"—in the grand manner:

> And therefore I have sailed the seas and come
> To the holy city of Byzantium.

But "once out of nature," in the last stanza, implies that, not yet in the holy city, he must be on its dock or porch, waiting. The sages, coming out of eternal mosaic and fire, must re-enter time to prepare his heart and soul for admission. "Once out of nature" or dead, the old man will be gone into just the paradise for him—no love or nature around, but plenty of courtiers to sing to. This is one possible reading of the poem. Another is to find its theme the making of a work of art:

[32]

bird, song, man, and the other things of nature, transfigured, become the unnatural golden bird, seated on Vergil's golden bough in Turner's picture. Like Keats's Grecian urn, the golden bird is beyond change—gold is the most stable of metals. But as the urn, out of time, brings news of a time, so the timeless bird sings of time, "Of what is past, or passing, or to come." The work of art, uniting timelessness with time, is an escape from time. Proust's novel makes this point and so, in a way, does Andrew Marvell's garden, a formal paradise with silver bird. Not garden, however, but voyage or journey provides the frame for Yeats's poem, an "archetypal" pattern that Joyce, Dante, and Homer had found useful. Nothing better and more customary for encounters with life, death, and, sometimes, art.

After experiment with Cowley's stanza and other "forms of intensity," Yeats had settled upon ottava rima. Any tight stanza gave him the desired tension between formal limits and the syntax of speech, between the grand and the natural; but ottava rima, bringing a comic air from Ariosto and Byron, added, when turned to serious ends, a further tension that Yeats, the student of interacting opposites, found agreeable. Moreover, the terminal couplet of ottava rima, with its grandeur and finality, allows a triumph of sound and rhythm. Such triumphs bring "Sailing to Byzantium" from climax to climax until the final stanza, climax of all four. This structure of triumphs and conflicts is tightened by motifs—as of bird and song. Indeed, the parts consort well with one another. That this work of art is the product of labor and great craft —"an intense unnatural labour that reduces composition to four or five lines a day"—is proved by the manuscripts of the poem in process, than which there is no better picture of the craftsman at work.

Lacking the assurance of ottava rima, "Byzantium" also misses the monumental magnificence of its predecessor, though theme and many images are the same. Souls come to the purgatory of phase 15 to rid themselves of time or the wheel's complexities; so too from the complexities of nature comes the work of art. "Image," purged or unpurged, covers soul and work alike. Images that "fresh images beget" without hope of finality are the danger. Since the purged, unified, and final image is his desire, it is strange that Yeats used two images, smithy and dancing floor, for what one image seems enough. Dome, mosaic, and golden bird are the poem's matter. The dancing floor is mosaic and the smithy is for golden birds, but neither golden-bird factory nor floor seems a proper breakwater. Flood and sea are time and complexity, through which dolphins bear their candidates. Rejected for "Sailing to Byzantium," the traditional image of the man-bearing dolphin demanded inclusion here—luckily; for it is the most memorable part of the poem. That the dolphins' port is not altogether ideal is suggested by the whores and drunks who throng it before closing time. The curfew from St. Sophia, announcing the purity of midnight, also torments the image-begetting sea. "All mere complexities" must endure the disdain of the purged and final image—pure, single, and eternal, whether soul or work of art.

Commending unity, "Among School Children" also ends with two images where one should do. But the rivalry of chestnut tree and dancer seems all but justifiable: the tree may stand for unity of nature; the dancer, hardly ever standing, embodies the unity of art. Both tree and dancer involve time and creation. The blossomer bears nuts, but who knows what the dancer bears? At once final and unfinal, the question mark at the end says more or less than we think.

Ottava rima contends again with turbulence of rhythm and sound—sometimes even in the final couplet of the stanza:

> A compensation for the pang of his birth,
> Or the uncertainty of his setting forth?

Yet, as Yeats desired, there is "complete coincidence between period and syntax" and uncommon firmness of structure. The poem advances logically and passionately from a
quiet opening, through a time of agitation, to the appeasing,
inevitable end. The interlocking parts seem no less inevitable;
yet "paradigm" (in stanza VI), the necessary echo of the
schoolroom (in stanza I) is an afterthought, not there in the
first printing.

A senatorial inspection of a school demands commonplace
language; but "In the best modern way"—what the good nun
said—is elevated above the commonplace by irony. Not even
this, however, diminishes the sudden drama of youth con-
fronting sixty years. Age and missing "the yolk and white of
the one shell" become the theme. The "Ledaean body" is that
of young Maud Gonne, Yeats's Helen—Ledaean because Helen
was hatched from one of those two eggs. As Maud, old now,
took, when young, "a mess of shadows" for her meat, so, in
their ways, nuns, mothers, and philosophers have taken
shadows for subsistence. Each astray in some egg-headed enterprise, Plato, solider Aristotle, and Pythagoras are nothing
more than old scarecrows. (Magnanimous Yeats, the "com-
fortable," smiling scarecrow of stanza IV, belongs in their
company.) Mothers, nuns, and philosophers, deluded by
images, need this advice:

> Labour is blossoming or dancing where
> The body is not bruised to pleasure soul,
> Nor beauty born out of its own despair,
> Nor blear-eyed wisdom out of midnight oil.
> O chestnut-tree, great-rooted blossomer,
> Are you the leaf, the blossom or the bole?
> O body swayed to music, O brightening glance,
> How can we know the dancer from the dance?

This poem, Yeats said, is his "curse upon old age." But what
he needed to make him great was growing old.

Rage at growing old, displacing ideas of unity, directs his

[35]

advice to the old girls of Lissadell, Eva Gore-Booth and Con Markiewicz, who, though from a great house with a large garden, ate shadows too:

> The innocent and the beautiful
> Have no enemy but time.

For the language of rage—for heroic defiance of our enemy—we must go to "The Lamentation of the Old Pensioner," a poem of 1890 or thereabouts. Young Yeats wrote:

> The well-known faces are all gone:
> And the fret lies on me.

Coming upon these lines in 1924, old Yeats rewrote them:

> I spit into the face of Time
> That has transfigured me.

These words could have been spoken by Crazy Jane herself, whose words ("for music perhaps") begin the last period. Less abundance here than in the previous decade, but the best poems from 1932 to 1939, the year of Yeats's death, are as good as most in *The Tower:* some of the songs, "Lapis Lazuli," "The Circus Animals' Desertion," and that great epitaph. Meditations in ottava rima continue the old magnificence. But the poems that are of this time entirely have the lustiness and gaiety, the ease and power of a "wild old wicked man." What wisdom age confers made common speech and natural syntax commoner and more natural—within limits. A poet must think like a wise man, Yeats said, and express himself like the common people. Unable, however wise he was, to find unity in life, he had settled for unity in art. "The Choice" (1931), with its extremities of logical abstraction and terrible particulars, suddenly meeting, makes his choice and its consequences plain:

> The intellect of man is forced to choose
> Perfection of the life, or of the work,
> And if it take the second must refuse
> A heavenly mansion, raging in the dark.

Lady Gregory died in 1932. They established a sawmill in the Seven Woods and tore the great house down. To take the place of Lady Gregory, Coole, and all that "lost tradition," Lady Dorothy Wellesley provided flowering lawns, in England. (Mrs. Yeats tolerantly stayed at home.) Editing *The Oxford Book of Modern Verse* brought Yeats face to face with Auden and those whose "intricate density" seemed a departure from Yeats's road of "naturalness and swiftness." T. S. Eliot's "flatness" still displeased; not so Edith Sitwell's "passion ennobled by intensity." Yeats devoted nineteen pages of the Oxford anthology to Dame Edith, seventeen pages to Lady Dorothy, who wrote poetry too, and fourteen to T. S. Eliot. Increasing infirmity drove Yeats to winter at Rapallo (with Ezra Pound) and Majorca. He wrote plays to keep his lyrics warm. To warm his imagination he consorted with a swami, the "homely precisions" of whose Indian thought proved as agreeable as Dame Edith's bones. "It looks," said Yeats, "as if I may have a spirited old age."

The Crazy Jane poems, begun in Rapallo in 1929, "praise joyous life," he said, but not that of great houses now; for he had exchanged the mask of the courtier for that of the fool—and the vagrant. (Yeats had in mind an old trot he once had words with on a road near Gort.) Crazy Jane's songs, personal and distant, owe their crab-apple tartness not only to "audacious" speech, dissonance, irregular rhythm, and off-key refrains, but to the wisdom of age. Jane may be mad or foolish, but, having lived, she knows that love, made of contending opposites, is a union of body and soul—of "fair and foul," as well; for "Love has pitched his mansion in / The place of excrement." A fool's wisdom gets to the bottom of things. But the method of getting there detained Edith Sitwell. The dissonance of "would" and "God," in "Crazy Jane on God," plunged that student of texture "into unmeasurable depths";

[37]

"house" and "ruinous" gave her "a feeling of huddled misery." Such impressions—blameless and instructive—led her to a judgment: these fusions of spirit and matter, she said, are "undoubtedly the greatest lyrics of the last hundred years." As for Yeats: never had writing come more easily. Maybe instead of four or five lines a day he now wrote six or seven. Reading what he had so easily composed, he found it "exciting and strange."

Although the speakers of text and refrain in "Crazy Jane Reproved" are uncertain, it is likely that the refrain is Jane's and the text, pointing to a connection of love and art, is the poet's. The extremes of love and art, Yeats tells Jane, may be roaring violence and painful delicacy but the latter is better:

> Great Europa played the fool
> That changed a lover for a bull.

To Jane's irreverent *"Fol de rol,"* he replies:

> To round that shell's elaborate whorl,
> Adorning every secret track
> With the delicate mother-of-pearl,
> Made the joints of Heaven crack.

Her refrains, here and elsewhere, her derangement of matters, and her violations of the customary have the "irrational element" that Yeats, with "Sing a Song of Sixpence" in mind, thought poetry must have.

Among the poems that immediately follow Crazy Jane's are several more that Yeats spoke with the masks of women on—women of four kinds: one a bone now on the shore, one a mother nursing child, one an oracle on her tripod, and one (young or old) a student of love. "Three Things" and "Lullaby" seemed to Yeats, as they must seem to us, among his best things: nothing so clear and public, nothing with more tenderness and greater humanity. The bone on the shore sings of remembered flesh—of giving suck, of making love, and of relaxing after it: "O cruel Death, give three things back." (A lesser bone, or one without Yeats around, might have sung:

give back three things.) The final dissonance of "man" and "yawn" embodies, perhaps, this bone's sense of lacking body now. In "Lullaby" the singer has her body on. But how odd to put her child to sleep with songs of Paris, Tristram, and Leda's Swan—all sleepy to be sure; but the sleep that comes after making love is nothing to tell a child about, however sleepy the rhythm of the telling:

> Roe could run or doe could leap
> Under oak and beechen bough,
> Roe could leap or doe could run.

Tender and humane maybe, old Yeats was grotesque as well. Singing bone and amorous lullaby are good examples of this; but there is no plainer example than "The Delphic Oracle upon Plotinus." The original of this short poem is a long one composed by the Delphic Oracle herself, to be found in Porphyry's life of Plotinus. By selecting and condensing Yeats made a poem out of her diffuse stuff. But the grotesque figure of "that great Plotinus" swimming through the sea of time toward the "choir of Love," beckoning on some Elysian shore, is oracular. A Delphic fancy, exciting the lover of voyages to harmonious nowheres, gave him the thought of doing "Byzantium" over, more compendiously.

The sixth poem of "A Woman Young and Old" points to the auspices under which Yeats's women sang of flesh and bone or body and soul in masculine language. For such conjunctions of the physical and the metaphysical Yeats had turned to John Donne again. "Chosen," the sixth song of this suite, is composed in the stanza of Donne's "A nocturnall upon S. Lucies day," and the final image of zodiac becoming sphere is a learned conceit of time and eternity. But for the metaphysical poems that follow this, written under Hindu auspices, a swami seemed more suitable than Donne.

Not body and soul but "sex and soul" provided theme for "Supernatural Songs." In these poems Ribh (Reeve), an Irish saint, prefers the Emerald Tablet of Hermes Trismegistus to St. Patrick's Trinity. As above, so below, however, is less his concern than as below, so above, where the gods enjoy man's "sexual spasm." Other more enigmatic poems—one astrological, another lunar—refer to the doctrine of the wheel that Yeats was busy improving. "The Four Ages of Man," according to a letter, uses the four elements as symbols of the phases man must go through. This and other poems need explanatory letters; for never were poems less "public." But maybe he had the mask of a saint on.

Good that, taking it off for good, he put on another, the mask of "the wild old wicked man" now. *The Arabian Nights*, Rabelais, and Swift crowded the Upanishads off his bedside table. Sheherazade, Yeats said, says "it is not shameful to talk of the things that lie beneath our belts": so he began to make the private public again. His old age, fired anew by "lust and rage," demanded appropriate song: "Come swish around, my pretty punk." He had news for the Delphic Oracle: Plotinus, Pythagoras, and all those "golden codgers" now sigh for love on the once Elysian shore, where:

> Belly, shoulder, bum,
> Flash fishlike; nymphs and satyrs
> Copulate in the foam.

The sighing for love that Yeats and his Plotinus knew also accounts for "The Lover's Song," than which no happier effect of greater economy of means. "Sighs" and "rest" are the poles. Let the poem be our sphere. Bird, thought, and seed fall sighing to rest through the suspended rhyme of the third line and the penultimate retardation of "straining," the only word of more than one syllable. Meanwhile, the movement rises from three beats to four, then falls to two. What these means—and others—have to do with the effect somebody, someday, must figure out.

[40]

Clarity and strength also distinguish the social and political poems that, in the political 1930s, Yeats was unable to defer. His romantic Ireland dead and gone, he saw "increasing commonness" around him. Base blood had driven the better out and riches, rank. Lacerated by Swift's "savage indignation," he wrote ballads, for singing in the streets perhaps, on the betrayers of Parnell and the forgers of Casement's diaries. He praised Pearse, Connolly, and The O'Rahilly—Cuchulain's rivals—killed at or near the Post Office in 1916. "The Curse of Cromwell," one of the best of these, may seem even more remote from the cares of the 1930s, but it was Cromwell who, burning great houses down and killing horsemen, brought democratic commonness in. As Auden was a little to the left of center, so Yeats was a little to the right. For O'Duffy's Blue Shirts, off to help Franco in Spain, he wrote marching songs, which he moderated when he found O'Duffy's "heroic dream" no better than democracy. Giving the whole thing up, holding his detestable time "at arm's length," he cursed Moscow, Rome, and Spain. As for Ireland—every garret and cellar crowded with communists or Catholics and every street with journalists: "My hatred tortures me with love, my love with hatred." Knowing he could not bring Cuchulain back, he settled for a return to the eighteenth century, "a greater, a more gracious time" when, with Swift and Berkeley around, the "lovers of horses and of women" enjoyed what great houses Cromwell had left standing. In "The Gyres," a lament for our bloody time, he awaits with confidence the coming round again of this "unfashionable gyre." Waiting its turn, he wrote poems—"John Kinsella's Lament," for example—in the manner he had learned from Frank O'Connor and F. R. Higgins, whose translations from eighteenth-century Gaelic rival Swift's "astringent eloquence."

Two images haunted Yeats these days: the horseman again

and the ruined house, lit up at night and tenanted by ghosts. Horseman and house show all his nostalgia for aristocracy, but the house also shows his awareness of present decline. These obsessive images appear in poem after poem, the horseman, at last, in his epitaph and the house in *Purgatory*, his penultimate play, "a scene," he said, "of tragic intensity."

The state of Ireland is but a distraction to an arranger of words. Modern letters, like modern politics, seemed sunk in flux, a deluge of subjective experience without limits, in which man is a swimmer or a wave. Bergson had "turned the world into fruit salad." Taking a stand with Wyndham Lewis, the champion of space against time, Yeats devoted *Fighting the Waves*, play and preface, to the humanist's heroic, but hopeless, battle with Bergson and his "filthy modern tide." In "The Statues," "plummet-measured" form opposes "Asiatic vague immensities." Cuchulain, in both play and poem, embodies man's measured refusal to be swallowed up. Art may be the triumph of measurement, but in "Long-Legged Fly" measurement, beyond intellect, seems work of the nonchalant hand or of inadvertence. Caesar, an artist in affairs, Helen, an artist and an artifact, and Michael Angelo create forms in the way a long-legged fly, kept above depths by surface tension, walks on, not in, the Bergsonian stream. Not that painter's mind but "his hand moves to and fro" on a surface.

"Lapis Lazuli," the great poem about art and the artist, is one that poets—Dylan Thomas and Robert Lowell among them—liked or like to read aloud without comment. Indeed, there seems little call for words beyond these: that none but a man whose words obeyed his call could have put the thing together. Yet, a few inobedient words seem called for here. The poem falls into three interacting parts: first, the occasion, second, a discourse, and third, an exemplary narrative that brings "measured quietude" to troubled thesis and antithesis.

[42]

Never better than in the opening lines had Yeats used the very words, rhythm, sound, and syntax—these overheard at some cocktail party—of common speech; and never had he shaped such matter better or heightened it with greater craft (except maybe in the first stanza of "Among School Children"):

> I have heard that hysterical women say
> They are sick of the palette and fiddle-bow,
> Of poets that are always gay,
> For everybody knows or else should know
> That if nothing drastic is done
> Aeroplane and Zeppelin will come out,
> Pitch like King Billy bomb-balls in
> Until the town lie beaten flat.

"Sick of" and "drastic" are the necessary prelude to King Billy's explosion.

In the second part, artists, knowing no "handiwork" can stand for long, welcome with gaiety its remaking. (Gaiety is what Mozart had.) The answer to those women yields now to the serene finale. "Accomplished fingers" playing, three Chinamen, in a work of art, stare from their mountain at the tragic scene below. Their gaiety, from accomplishment in part, comes also from playing things as they are, at a distance.

Poems of memory and meditation, always self-estimates, are either complacent or bitter now. In "The Municipal Gallery Revisited," a memory of the first kind, Yeats congratulates himself, magnanimously, on his friends and the glory he has acquired from having them. It was he, together with Lady Gregory and Synge, who, finding virtue in "the common tongue," gave words to nobleman and beggar. But "The Apparitions" is not complacent at all. Here, the estimate of self concentrates in the refrain: a vision—the worst of fifteen he has had—of "a coat upon a coat-hanger," an image, more terrible than the scarecrow of "Sailing to Byzantium," that brings to mind embroidered coat and mask. Most terrible of all,

[43]

however, is "The Circus Animals' Desertion." Beginning quietly enough in the everyday words that he was master of, he takes his heart for theme, the heart's displays—its circus animals on show—and the heart itself. "Oisin," *The Countess Cathleen*, and *On Baile's Strand*, the displays he picks from a life of displaying, were heart's truth perhaps, but the works themselves "And not those things that they were emblems of" enchanted him. Now the examination goes deeper: what, after all, was the heart out of which "those masterful images" came?

> A mound of refuse or the sweepings of a street,
> Old kettles, old bottles, and a broken can,
> Old iron, old bones, old rags, that raving slut
> Who keeps the till. Now that my ladder's gone,
> I must lie down where all the ladders start,
> In the foul rag-and-bone shop of the heart.

However accustomed we are to pity and fear, these lines move us—even more than those on our time in "The Second Coming." Mr. Krook's rag, bottle, and bone shop in *Bleak House* is less disheartening because less our own affair. Maybe the only comparable vision of our hearts is Conrad's *Heart of Darkness*.

Above the ladders' start, "Under Ben Bulben" (1938), grand and bare as the mountain itself, is the "gist" of what his sages, horsemen, and women "mean"—of all, in short, Yeats meant—of life, of death, of country and art. "Learn your trade," he tells Irish poets; sing the well-made song of "whatever is well made." Sing "the indomitable Irishry": the horsemen, peasants, saints, and drunks, the lords and ladies of "seven heroic centuries." What matter that no poet has taken his advice? His epitaph is example enough of what a poet can do:

> *Cast a cold eye*
> *On life, on death.*
> *Horseman, pass by!*

What matter that no nonchalant horsemen—only middle-class tourists in taxis—pass that churchyard by nowadays? There, cut in stone, is what Yeats stood for, put in a way to make the chills run down your spine: all that distance and nobility, all that craft.

SELECTED BIBLIOGRAPHY

NOTE: *The principal works of Yeats, with the exception of his letters, have all been published by The Macmillan Company, London and New York.*

For a complete bibliography, see Allan Wade: A Bibliography of the Writings of W. B. Yeats. *London, Rupert Hart-Davis, 1951; revised edition, 1958.*

PRINCIPAL WORKS OF W. B. YEATS

A Vision. London, 1937; New York, 1938 (also in paperback).

Letters on Poetry from W. B. Yeats to Dorothy Wellesley. London, Oxford University Press, 1940.

The Collected Poems. London, 1950; New York, 1951.

The Collected Plays. London, 1952; New York, 1953.

Autobiography. New York, 1953 (also in paperback).

W. B. Yeats: Letters to Katharine Tynan. Edited by Roger McHugh. Dublin, Clonmore and Reynolds, 1953.

W. B. Yeats and T. Sturge Moore: Their Correspondence. Edited by Ursula Bridge. London, Routledge, 1953.

The Letters of W. B. Yeats. Edited by Allan Wade. London, Rupert Hart-Davis, 1954. [The introductions constitute the best brief biography of Yeats.]

Autobiographies. London, 1955.

The Variorum Edition of the Poems. Edited by Peter Allt and Russell K. Alspach. New York, 1957.

Mythologies. London, 1959; New York, 1959.

Essays and Introductions. London, 1961; New York, 1961.

Explorations. London, 1962; New York, 1963.

Selected Poems. Edited by M. L. Rosenthal. New York, 1962 (a paperback).

CRITICAL WORKS AND COMMENTARY

Bradford, Curtis. Yeats at Work. Carbondale, Southern Illinois University Press, 1965.

Bradford, Curtis. "Yeats's Byzantium Poems: A Study of Their Development." *PMLA*, LXXV (March, 1960), 110–25.

Ellmann, Richard. The Identity of Yeats. New York, Oxford University Press, 1954.

——— Yeats, the Man and the Masks. New York, Macmillan, 1948.

Engelberg, Edward. The Vast Design. Patterns in W. B. Yeats's Aesthetic. Toronto, University of Toronto Press, 1965.

Exhibition Catalogue: W. B. Yeats, Images of a Poet. Manchester, University of Manchester Press, 1961.

Gonne, Maud. A Servant of the Queen. Reminiscences. London, Victor Gollancz, 1938.

Hall, James, and Martin Steinman, eds. The Permanence of Yeats: Selected Criticism. New York, Macmillan, 1950.

Henn, T. R. The Lonely Tower: Studies in the Poetry of W. B. Yeats. London, Methuen, 1950.

Hone, Joseph. W. B. Yeats, 1865–1939. New York, Macmillan, 1943.

Jeffares, A. Norman. W. B. Yeats, Man and Poet. New Haven, Yale University Press, 1949.

——— ed. In Excited Reverie. A Centenary Tribute to William Butler Yeats. London, Macmillan, 1965.

Kermode, Frank. Romantic Image. London, Routledge, 1957.

Moore, George. Hail and Farewell. New York, Appleton, 1925.

Moore, Virginia. The Unicorn: William Butler Yeats' Search for Reality. New York, Macmillan, 1954.

Nathan, Leonard. Figures in a Dance: William Butler Yeats' Development as a Tragic Dramatist, 1884–1939. New York, Columbia University Press, 1965.

Parkinson, Thomas. W. B. Yeats, Self-Critic. Berkeley, University of California Press, 1951.

——— W. B. Yeats: the Later Poetry. Berkeley, University of California Press, 1965.

Parrish, Stephen Maxfield. A Concordance to the Poems of W. B. Yeats. Ithaca, Cornell University Press, 1963.

Rajan, Balachandra. W. B. Yeats. A Critical Introduction. London, Hutchinson, 1965.

Saul, George Brandon. Prolegomena to the Study of Yeats's Poems. Philadelphia, University of Pennsylvania Press, 1957.

Saul, George Brandon. Prolegomena to the Study of Yeats's Plays. Philadelphia, University of Pennsylvania Press, 1958.

Seiden, Morton. William Butler Yeats, the Poet as a Mythmaker. East Lansing, Michigan State University Press, 1962.

Stauffer, Donald. The Golden Nightingale. New York, Macmillan, 1949.

Stock, A. G. W. B. Yeats: his Poetry and Thought. Cambridge, Cambridge University Press, 1961.

Unterecker, John. A Reader's Guide to William Butler Yeats. New York, Noonday Press, 1959.

———ed. Yeats: A Collection of Critical Essays. Englewood Cliffs, New Jersey, Prentice-Hall, 1963.

Ure, Peter. Yeats, the Playwright. New York, Barnes & Noble, 1963.

Wilson, F. A. C. W. B. Yeats and Tradition. New York, Macmillan, 1958.

——— Yeats's Iconography. New York, Macmillan, 1960.

Winters, Yvor. The Poetry of W. B. Yeats. Denver, Colorado, Allan Swallow, 1960.

Yeats, J. B. Letters to His Son W. B. Yeats and Others, 1869–1922. Edited by Joseph Hone. London, Faber, 1944.

Tindall, William York, 1903-
 W. B. Yeats.   New York, Columbia University
Press, 1966.
 48 p.   (Columbia essays on modern writers,
no. 15)

 1. Yeats, William Butler, 1865-1939.   I.
Series.